Courageous Cora & The Brave Boys

JoAn Stevenson

by JoAn Stevenson

with illustrations by Kayla Olson-Surface

TEACUP  PRESS

www.teacup-press.com
www.foxpointepublishing.com/author-jo-an-stevenson

Library of Congress Cataloging-in-Publication Data
Stevenson, JoAn, author.
Farr, Chelsea, editor.
Olson-Surface, Kayla, illustrator.
Farr, Chelsea, designer.
Courageous Cora & The Brave Boys / JoAn Stevenson. – First edition.
Summary: A group of boys and their dragon assist a princess with her escape plan from an ogre.
ISBN 978-1-955743-04-4 (hardcover) / 978-1-955743-05-1 (softcover)
[1. Action & Adventure – Fiction. 2. Friendship – Fiction. 3. Dragons – Fiction.]
Library of Congress Control Number: 2 0 2 2 9 4 1 2 6 7

Printed and bound in the United States of America by Lakeside Press Inc.
First printing August 2022

This book is dedicated to all children who believe in fairytales, old and new.
Always be brave and kind.

To my five children and all my grandchildren who inspire me.

To Emma, Gigi, Vivian, Odan, Greta, Una, Emmett, and Elliana.
If you promise to keep reading then I will keep writing stories for you!

To my granddaughter, Cora, the courageous, young princess.

To the five brave boys who are my grandsons:
Avery, Nicholas, Evan, Liam, and Elan.

To my grandson, Finlay, the fearless dragon.

And to my mother, Lorene Conner, who encouraged me to write poetry
which developed into children's stories.

Once upon a time
in a land far away...
I will tell you a tale
of some kids who
were brave.

The littlest was Elan;
he was kind and wise
and he never worried
about his small size.

    The strongest was Liam;
the bravest was Evan.
They were courageous and bold
and had both just turned seven.

Their big brothers were
called Avery and Nick.
So smart and clever,
those two knew many a trick!

3

It happened one morning
down by the shore
that Fin, their fierce dragon,
let out a great roar!

4

"What is it?" said Evan.
"A bottle!" said Nick.
"There's a map with a note—
come on, read it quick!"

5

Please help me!

Come as quick as you can!

I've been captured by an ogre
with the most evil plan!

He is humongous, mean,
smelly, and hairy!

He wants my pet hen
and that is quite scary!

The silver eggs my hen lays
are the reason, I'd guess...

I sure hope you can
help me out
of this mess!

In a moss-covered tower
I am utterly stuck!

It is boring, quite dreadful,
and very high up!

I've come up with a plan—
please accept this quest.

Come distract the ogre,
I'll take care of the rest!

Princess Cora
wrote the note—
she was clever, strong,
and brave,
and if her daring plan
worked,
she and her hen would
be saved.

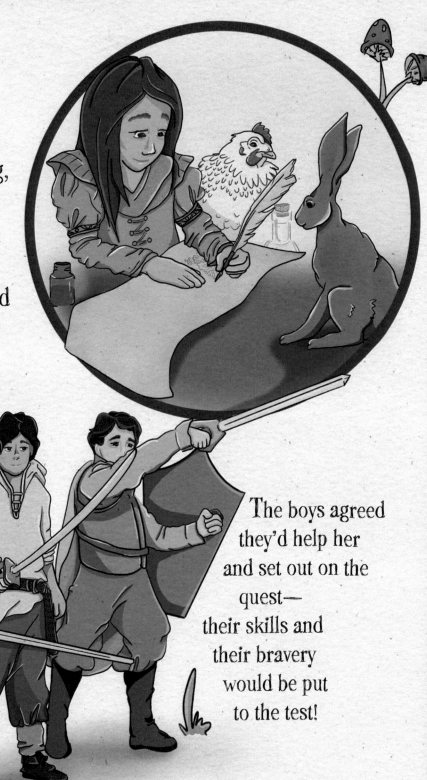

The boys agreed
they'd help her
and set out on the
quest—
their skills and
their bravery
would be put
to the test!

They dropped by their secret cave
to gather up some supplies.
The bad ogre would be in
for an interesting surprise!

Fin and the boys arrived
   and as they crept toward the tower,
   they could already smell the ogre—
Oh, how he needed a shower!

The ogre was quite surprised
to see them just then—
but he wasn't about
to give up that prize hen!

12

"You can't have them!"
snarled the ogre,
and he meant what he said!
His huge fists were clenched
and his face turned bright red.

13

Nicholas said, "Play some calm music—
we will trick the big brute!"

Liam reached in his pocket
and pulled out
his golden flute.

"Get your slingshots out, boys!"
whispered Avery.
"Magic jelly beans might
also work!"
So they reached in
their rucksacks
and took aim at
the big jerk.

15

Then the flute could be heard,

and the beans were sent soaring.

The ogre gobbled
up the candy,

CHOMPING
and
ROARING!

Then the magic music took hold
and the ogre gave a mighty yawn.
He smacked his lips, patted his belly,
and fell fast asleep on the lawn.

17

Princess Coralin appeared
    at the tower window just then.
"Fantastic job, all of you!
Let's bring this quest to an end."

She then tossed down a net
    that landed with a thump!
The boys stretched it out
    and the princess did jump.

Avery whistled for Fin,
who had hid in the brush.

"Step lively, my pet,
as we do need to rush!"

They climbed on his back
and soon skimmed
the trees,
as the ogre awoke
and started to sneeze.

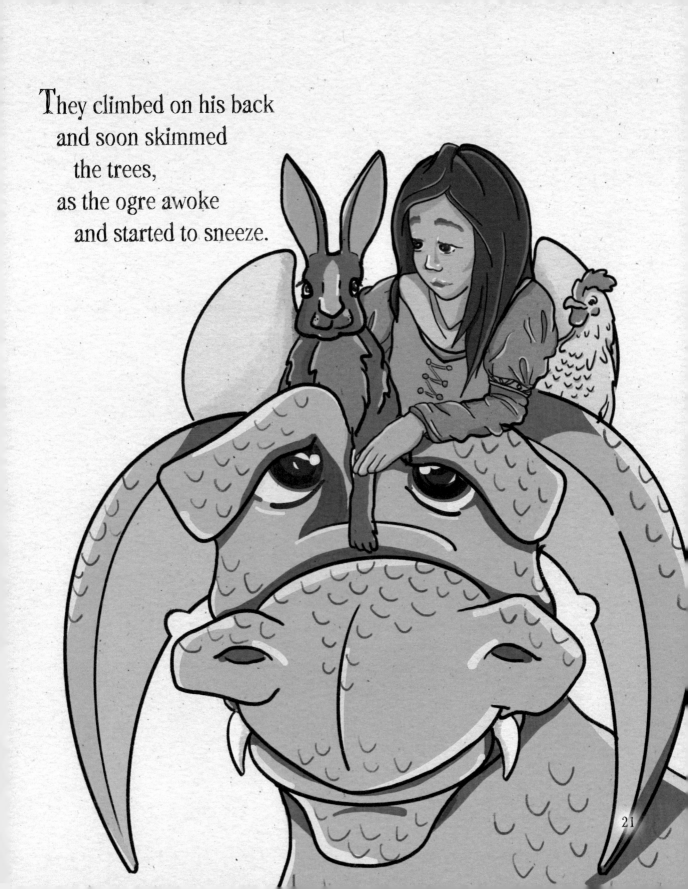

They talked about their
great adventure
and the strange dreams
they'd have that night.

They were laughing
when they landed
at the third kingdom
on the right.

23

Said the King and Queen,
"Thanks for helping Cora—
  we've missed her so much!
You must be quite hungry!
Please stay for a royal lunch!"

After, the boys strapped on their swords,
then bowed and waved to the people.
With the boys on his back,
Fin flew into the sky,
up, up, up, high above
the church steeple.

The princess soon
  looked quite small,
then dropped completely
  out of sight.
"Let's head home,
  it's very late—
we have fought
  the good fight!"

My tale is now told;
   the story is quite true!
The boys headed for home—
   they were long overdue.

                    Princess Cora and the boys
                        had become fast friends;
                    this is where their first
                        adventure ends...

JoAn Stevenson is a fifth-generation Iowan and is now beginning a retirement career of writing books, mainly in the genres of children's and poetry. She has always been an avid reader and believes this is why she took up writing decades ago. Every year, she and her family members submit poems to the annual publication, "Lyrical Iowa."

JoAn has five children and several grandchildren. She lives with three cats and enjoys reading, knitting, traveling, cooking, gardening, biking, and volunteering. Her favorite color is blue and she adores apple pie, Italian food, and potatoes in any form!